JOURNEY WITHIN

Balboa Press books may be ordered through booksellers or by contacting:

Balboa Press
A Division of Hay House
1663 Liberty Drive
Bloomington, IN 47403
www.balboapress.com
844-682-1282

Because of the dynamic nature of the Internet, any web addresses or links contained in this book may have changed since publication and may no longer be valid. The views expressed in this work are solely those of the author and do not necessarily reflect the views of the publisher, and the publisher hereby disclaims any responsibility for them.

The author of this book does not dispense medical advice or prescribe the use of any technique as a form of treatment for physical, emotional, or medical problems without the advice of a physician, either directly or indirectly. The intent of the author is only to offer information of a general nature to help you in your quest for emotional and spiritual well-being. In the event you use any of the information in this book for yourself, which is your constitutional right, the author and the publisher assume no responsibility for your actions.

Any people depicted in stock imagery provided by Getty Images are models, and such images are being used for illustrative purposes only. Certain stock imagery © Getty Images.

Cover photo by, Trevor Bonderud/First Light "Path Through Trees in Mist".

Print information available on the last page.

ISBN: 978-1-9822-7559-4 (sc)

Balboa Press rev. date: 02/23/2022

Journey Within

A PATH TO INNER PEACE

K.J. SIMMONS

BALBOA.PRESS

A DIVISION OF HAY HOUSE

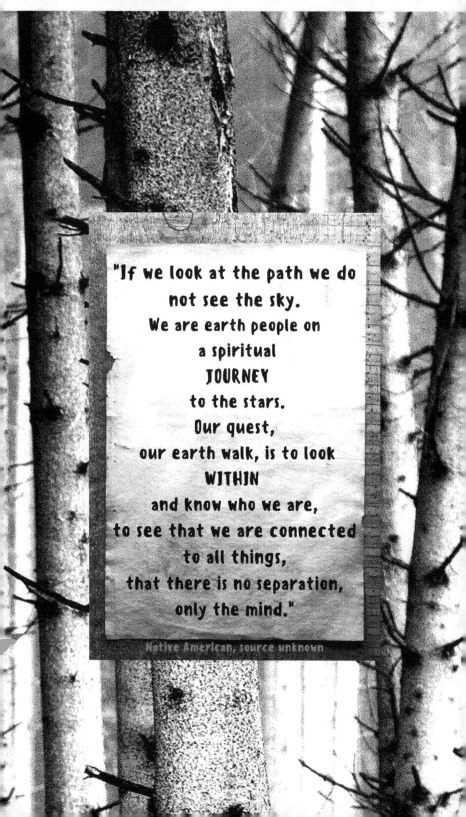

" IF ALL YOU CAN DO IS CRAWL

START CRAWLING."

RUMI, 13TH-CENTURY PERSIAN POET

CONTENTS

"FOR THINGS TO REVEAL THEMSELVES TO US,

WE NEED TO BE READY

TO ABANDON

OUR VIEWS ABOUT THEM."

THICH NHAT HANH, ZEN MASTER, BUDDHIST MONK

INTRODUCTION

Every minute of every day you are choosing your level of consciousness. Your thoughts are creating your reality. Being open to a shift in perception, seeing the world differently, is where this journey begins.

Inspired by the combined framework of Michael Bernard Beckwith and Mary O'Malley, I applied my life's journey as a guide for others to find their own inner peace. You must work through each level and process what has been revealed in order to elevate your consciousness. The levels are:

Life Happens TO You - The Victim
Life Happens BY You – The Storyteller/Control Freak
The YOU Turn – The Shift
Life Happens FOR You - Problems
Life Happens THROUGH You - Emotions
Life IS You - Connection
Life Is NOW – Present Moment

Journey Within is all about *you*. Its intention is to make you think, define who you are, and what you believe in. I purposely left out personal experiences because you will benefit more by connecting with your higher intelligence rather than trying to apply my advice to your life situation. This book is a *process*, so be patient and let it unfold.

There are no right or wrong answers because acknowledgment

is one of the big lessons in *Journey Within*. Not knowing what you feel, or what you think is part of the process. Don't answer a question if you don't know the answer. Reflect on your thoughts through journaling and answer when you have reached a conclusion. Be open to those conclusions changing throughout this journey.

Coloring has the same effect as meditation, reducing stress and creating the opportunity to shift to the right brain to experience peace and calmness. Use coloring as a way to relax and inspire your creative self. It's your world. Color it any color you like.

To begin the journey within, keep an open mind and let instincts and faith guide you. If you have never done this before, this book is an invitation to fearlessly hold your nose and jump. This never-ending journey of discovering who you are takes bravery as you work through the layers of life that have separated you from Source. Just keep taking steps forward and you will arrive at the desired destination, the Present Moment.

"EMPOWERMENT IS REALIZING YOU ARE THE ONE WHO NEEDS TO SAY THE THINGS YOU HAVE WAITED YOUR ENTIRE LIFE TO HEAR."

MATT KAHN, AUTHOR

DEDICATION

I dedicate this book to You.

I hope something in this book makes sense
to you. I hope it inspires you.
Even if you're well on your way in your spiritual
journey consider this book as a little reminder of
things you already knew but may have forgotten.
Most of all, I hope you don't see things quite the same way after
you have read it...that's my definition of enlightenment.
I intended this book to be a calling for you to take personal
responsibility and create the highest version of yourself.
I truly believe in my heart no matter where you are in
your life or what you've done, every 24 hours is another
opportunity to change direction, make a different choice.
The choice to be truly happy and find inner peace.
If you have not discovered your purpose in life, I
hope this book sets you on a path to find it.
As you heal yourself of whatever needs to be healed through
self-love and forgiveness, your inner flame will grow.
This journey within is about unearthing your Divine
Essence. Dig deep. Let your light shine.

With Love Always,
K.J. Simmons

Level One

LIFE HAPPENS TO YOU

Right now, you are sitting on the third rock from the Sun suspended by gravity, spinning at 1000 miles per hour in a vast inexplainable universe. It is an amazing concept, but the reality is our existence on planet earth can be uncertain. Most of us do not like thinking about life this way, but we never really know what is going to happen from day to day. Being creatures of habit, it is hard to accept that we have little control over our lives, and this can make us feel as though we are victims of circumstances beyond our control—and we are. It began the day you were born.

According to Dr. Bruce Lipton, Stem Cell Biologist, from birth to age seven you were exposed to the behavior, thoughts, and opinions of the people who raised you. During that time, your brain was operating at the theta brainwave stage, a slow, hypnotic state, and did not have the ability to create an opinion, a rational or critical thought, because your brain was developing other skills for your survival. Everything you learned about life were the experiences of other people and were downloaded into your subconscious mind. You did not choose this information; however, it was the foundation of how you see the world.

From the age of reason around 7 to 8 years old, and especially during the teen years, you may have felt the pangs of resistance as the first signs of who you truly are with what you were led to believe. Although most parents and caregivers have good intentions, they are people with their own struggles and can only parent from their level of consciousness. If you were subjected to a perspective that was negative, abusive, or distorted, the unconscious mind will accept whatever it is exposed to and believe this as truth. **What we believe becomes our reality.**

If we believe negative thoughts about ourselves that are internally generated by what we were told as children and young adults, this will lead to low self-esteem, creating victim mentality. Victim mentality is an acquired personality trait stemming from the concepts that we are not accountable nor responsible for our circumstances. As adults, this level of awareness manifests into needing endless attention and sympathy. Victims will create stories, reasons and explanations to justify not taking responsibility for their lives, keeping them in a constant state of lack.

It is impossible to change any behavior without first acknowledging it. It is equally as important to acknowledge how many of our thoughts are unconscious, repetitive, and unquestioned.

"You have the power over your mind—not outside events. Realize this and you will find strength."

Marcus Aurelius, Roman Emperor 161-180 CE

JOURNAL

It's YOUR Journey – Be the Narrator of YOUR life

Write your story with you as the main character using your first name. Do not use, "I", "me", or "my". Refer to the people in your story by their first name and "he/she".

1. Describe the environment you grew up in.

2. Describe your caregivers.

3. What were some of the things they said about you?

4. What is your very first memory? Good or bad.

    _____

    _____

    _____

    _____

5. Describe your childhood. Specifically, siblings, friends, school and interests.

    _____

    _____

    _____

    _____

    _____

6. Did you experience any trauma during your childhood? What was it?

    _____

    _____

    _____

    _____

    _____

7. Describe your adolescence through teen years. Specifically love interests and relationships. Write about the outstanding moments good and/or bad.

_____

_____

_____

_____

8. Describe the moment you felt you became an adult.

_____

_____

_____

_____

_____

9. Describe your life right now

_____

_____

_____

_____

_____

EXERCISE

Check off the statements that describe your (or someone else's) behavior. This exercise is not about blame. This is about acknowledgement, giving you to power to change and recognize victim behavior.

1. Someone with victim mentality constantly blames other people for who they have become, what they have become, and why they are in the situation they are in. _____

2. Victim mentality is the belief the world is against them, and people with this belief say things such as if they did not have bad luck, they would not have any luck at all. _____

3. Victims think people are against them and seek out support groups for sympathy as friends and family tire of their endless plight, and they end up being asked to leave the group. _____

4. Victim mentality is cynical and pessimistic. _____

5. People with victim mentality feel powerless to change their situation. _____

6. Victim mentality engages in "one-upmanship" with other Victims, competing on who has bigger or more problems. _____

7. Victims reinforce their victim mentality by telling their sad story to anyone who will listen, especially strangers. _____

8. Victims keep reliving and talking about their past, keeping them trapped in a constant state of victim mentality. _____

9. Victims feel singled out, as if they are the only one being targeted. _____

10. A person with victim mentality refuses to analyze their belief system, make changes to improve their life, and has a sense of entitlement. _____

11. Victims always have a reason, excuse or explanation as to why things never do work out, will never work out, or ever change for them. _____

13. Nothing ever seems to make Victims happy, they only experience temporary moments of joy and rarely show gratitude for what they have. _____

Own it and acknowledge it. Does any of this behavior sound familiar? Replace the word "victim" with the person who best suits the statement. Be mindful that the person might be you.

Why would anyone want to be a Victim?

Playing the Victim is all about attention. Two of the Victim's favorite forms of attention are praise and pity: praise for their endless self-sacrifice and pity when they complain about it. Victims create confrontation and thrive on drama because it is the "fuel" for their Victimhood. Victims need to be needed by someone or something. This attention gives them a false sense of purpose, keeping them trapped and creating victim mentality. Although the Victim is the first, lowest, and most dysfunctional level of consciousness, **victim mentality is extremely powerful because it works**. However, there is an underlying Victim who must be healed in order to achieve any lasting inner peace.

How and why victim mentality works.

- Victims crave attention and know how to get it.
- People sympathize with victims.
- People do not criticize victims as often as others.
- Some victims never deal with their emotions because they are just too sad.
- Their sadness (which usually leads to depression) keeps them in a place where people must continually help them financially, emotionally, or physically.
- People with victim mentality feel as though they have a right to complain.
- Victims are more likely to get what they want without really having to work for it.
- People with victim mentality are rarely bored because they constantly create drama.

- Victims believe they do not have to be responsible for anything: past, present, or future.
- Even though little ever changes in their lives, people with victim mentality think they are interesting and will tell their story over and over to anyone who will listen.

How are Victims created?

By feeling powerless and helpless. Powerlessness is an inability to enact choices. Helplessness is a sense of having no control. The Victim gives away all power the moment they believe other people's opinions are more important than their own and believe something outside themselves will make them happy.

JOURNAL

Based on the information provided in Level One, respond to the following questions.

1. Do you think you are a victim of your circumstances? How so?

   _____

   _____

   _____

   _____

2. Do you have some victim mentality? What is it?

   _____

   _____

   _____

   _____

3. Do you know where your victim mentality came from? Define the source

   _____

   _____

   _____

   _____

4. Do you know if your caregivers were victims of their circumstances? If so, what were they?

_____

_____

_____

_____

5. Now that you can recognize victim behavior, have you been unconsciously displaying it?

_____

_____

_____

_____

6. Now that you can recognize victim behavior, are there people in your life that act like victims? Name them.

_____

_____

_____

_____

"You are 0% responsible for the programming you received as a child, but as an adult you are 100% responsible for fixing it."

Author Unknown

How to heal the Victim.

The first step to change anything in your life is to acknowledge it. At the Victim level, you must begin to listen to the voice in your head and what it is saying all day long. **This is not you.** With thousands of thoughts running continuously through our minds, it is understandable that we become completely unaware of them. Some of the inner voice is intermingled with our thoughts and is generated from our subconscious. Part of the foundation for our subconscious are the opinions, criticisms, and ideas of other people; however, as adults we have the ability, choice, and responsibility to discern which are ours, which come from our past, and which come from an outside source and decide which to embrace. As you begin to listen to your thoughts, be especially mindful of self-sabotaging voices and their origins. Without judgment, see if any negative thoughts can be traced to a specific person, group, or experience from your past. As you become more conscious of what fills your mind, start to question which of these thoughts, opinions, criticisms, and judgments are your own. **Begin to define who you are and who you are not.**

Create a space between you and this voice. When self-criticism comes to mind, such as "you're not good enough or smart enough," question it. Is it an unconscious, repetitive thought you have been playing in your head and have come to believe? Begin to ask, "Who is saying I can't do this?" Figure out what generated that thought or doubt. Perhaps the truth is that you do not really have the desire, interest, or energy to make a change in your life. Or maybe, to avoid the emotion of failure, you allow your unconscious voice to convince you to not to even try something new or move in a different direction. **Being honest with yourself is essential to figuring out who you have become.**

As you become aware of your thoughts, you can focus on the positive and silence the negative. **Being the observer of your thoughts gives you the power to control them.**

When you start to recognize Victim behavior in yourself, you will begin to recognize it in others. Even if you were fortunate enough to be raised in a positive atmosphere where you felt loved and supported and think nothing but empowering thoughts about yourself, be mindful that victim mentality is an acquired personality trait that can develop later in life, usually after a traumatic event or series of continuous challenges. **Regardless of the reason a person is a Victim, it is their choice to live as one.**

Now that the voice in your head has a separate identity, you can begin to objectively listen (never judge) and start to **consciously change that dialogue.** You must determine what is true and what is not. **Higher consciousness begins when you figure out what you believe about yourself and what you do not, what you can change and what cannot.**

As you create a space to separate you from your thoughts, become aware of the things you are thinking about. Observe what flows in and out of your mind all day long and how unconscious and repetitive it is. **Controlling and directing your thoughts is one of the most powerful skills you can learn on your enlightened journey.** Begin to replace negative thoughts with consciousness: simple joys, quiet moments, and positive affirmations. **Your thoughts create your reality.**

Once the Victim realizes that their limiting beliefs, unconscious thoughts, and seeing life from a powerless position was **a reality of their own creation**, they want to make a change. As the Victim attempts to create a fulfilling life outside themselves, giving them great personal power, false control and shifting to the next level of awareness, the Storyteller is born.

"Don't take anything personally. Nothing others do is because of you. What others say is projection of their own reality, their own dream. When you are immune to the opinions of others, you won't be the victim of needless suffering."

Don Miguel Ruiz, Mexican author

Centering Thought

Today I am letting go of the Victim, victim mentality, and all negative thoughts from my past. Although I had no choice as a child, I have the power and responsibility as an adult to control my mind and find my own personal truth. In taking back my power, I forgive myself for believing thoughts that were not my own and commit to listening to my conscious voice so I can live in peace.

Daily Affirmation

I am not what happened to me.
I am what I chose to become.

"YOU ARE NOT A VICTIM.
NO MATTER WHAT YOU'VE BEEN THROUGH,
YOU'RE STILL HERE.
YOU MAY
HAVE BEEN
CHALLENGED,
HURT,
BETRAYED,
BEATEN, BUT
NOTHING
HAS
DEFEATED
YOU.
YOU ARE STILL HERE!
YOU HAVE BEEN DELAYED BUT NOT DENIED.
YOU ARE NOT A VICTIM BUT A VICTOR
YOU HAVE A HISTORY OF VICTORY."

STEVE MARIBOLI, AUTHOR

Journal

Journal

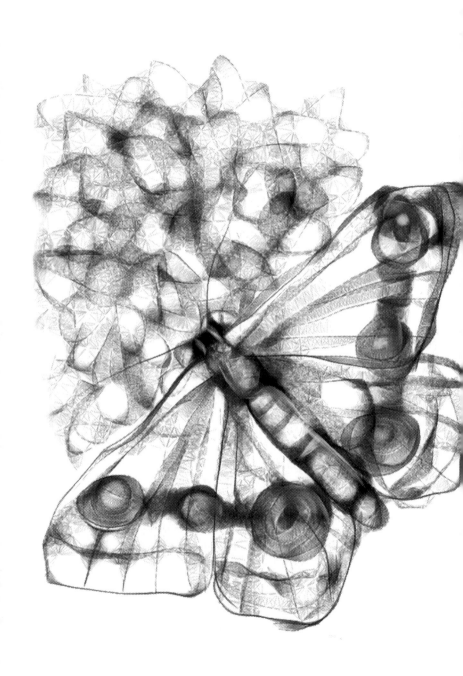

Level Two

LIFE HAPPENS BY YOU

Enough never seems to be enough. We have been conditioned to believe that things define who we are; a better job, a bigger house, or the latest technology, feeds the ego, giving the victim a false sense of empowerment. This is where the Victim is elevated to a Storyteller and the ego takes over their identity. Print ads, commercials, and internet sales are designed to convince us that "more is better". However, when the thrill of having the newest version of whatever they are selling wears off, the Storyteller will only be concerned with the next thing that gives them credibility, status, and the chance to be seen as the person who "has it all". Social media provides numerous platforms for the Storyteller to create an enviable version of themselves that provides the acceptance they need to feel good about who they are. The goal, which usually turns into an addiction, is to gain approval from many acquaintances rather than the loving support of just a few genuine relationships. Following celebrities on social media makes Storytellers feel connected, as if they know these people; when in fact, they are just inflating the egos and feeding the wallets of famous people.

"To be yourself in a world that is constantly trying to make you someone else, is the greatest accomplishment."

Ralph Waldo Emerson, American Essayist and philosopher

EXERCISE

Respond to the following statements. If you do not know the answer, begin to keep track, and then fill in the accurate response.

1. I check my social media status _____ times per hour.
2. I check my social media status _____ times per day.
3. I feel _____ when I get the response I was anticipating.
4. I feel _____ when I don't get the responses I was hoping for.
5. I can / cannot go for _____ minutes _____ hours _____ days without checking social media.
6. I am always _____ sometimes _____ never _____ honest about my life on social media.
7. I would _____ maybe _____ never _____ say the things I post in social media to someone's face.
8. If social media were to end tomorrow, I would feel _____.

"There are only two industries that call their customers "users". Illegal drugs and software."

Edward Tufte, American statistician

Why would anyone want to become a Storyteller?

Because relationships are difficult, complicated, and require effort, commitment, and forgiveness. Why bother when the ego can get fed on numerous social media platforms with the "click" of acceptance and approval on any issue or subject you want to create as your reality. Should the Storyteller not get the desired response, the post gets deleted. If there is conflict, the contact gets blocked. When the Storyteller is overwhelmed by responses, they take a break from social media, which usually is not long because the addiction to be accepted and followed by the masses has replaced the need for intimate relationships.

Storytellers who are not tech-savvy will attempt to re-create their past as the ego tries to relive a time when they felt better about themselves and were accepted by others. Reaching out to old friends and continuously talking about the "good old days" allows the storyteller to experience temporary feelings of worthiness that they are not experiencing in their current existence. This usually leaves them with a sense of hopelessness and longing for what was rather than accepting what is.

EXERCISE

Are you a storyteller? Be HONEST! Answer the questions and respond as to when or why you feel the way you do.

1. Do you care more about what other people think of you than what you think of yourself?

_____

_____

_____

_____

2. Do you change your personality and behavior to suit other people?

    _____

    _____

3. Do you adjust your personality or behavior to suit each situation?

    _____

    _____

4. Would you call yourself a "people pleaser"?

    _____

    _____

5. Do you do things you don't enjoy just so people will like and accept you?

    _____

    _____

6. Do you care for others before yourself?

    _____

    _____

As the Storyteller attempts to heal the Victim, the cost of maintaining the high level of attention necessary to feed the ego gets expensive, increasing their level of anxiety. At this point the Storyteller can revert to the victim level because they've created an image they can no longer afford, or they double down and become a Control Freak, or the You Turn begins.

What creates a Control Freak?

The fear of being controlled. Rather than addressing their own issues, the Control Freak attempts to control everyone around them, as well as every situation they are in. This false sense of superiority keeps their focus off what they lack and what other people have using financial, emotional, or physical control to maintain relationships.

Control Freak Behavior Checklist

EXERCISE

Check off the statement that describe your or someone else's behavior.

1. Must always win an argument and have the last word. _____
2. Refuse to admit they're wrong. _____
3. Critical and judgmental of other people. _____
4. Think they are 100 percent responsible for their own success. _____
5. They spend a lot of time convincing other people to change. _____
6. Refuse to apologize. _____
7. Have a difficult time maintaining relationships. _____
8. Do not like to delegate jobs or tasks. _____
9. Have no tolerance for mistakes and ridicule people when they make them. _____
10. Use anger or a "bad mood" to intimidate and emotionally control others. _____
11. Tend to be perfectionists. _____
12. Drive with rage. _____
13. Often redo the work of others. _____
14. Cannot handle criticism and respond angrily and defensively. _____

"There are two ways of being unhappy.
Not getting what you want is one.
Getting what you want is the other."

Eckhart Tolle. Spiritual Leader and author

What do the Storyteller and a Control Freak have in common?

Both the Storyteller and Control Freak are personality traits that are the result of low self-esteem. Low self-esteem is the byproduct of the victim due to a painful, unaddressed past.

How to heal the Storyteller.

To heal the Storyteller, you must come to the realization that **nothing outside of you will make you happy.** Material things feed the ego, sending the Storyteller on the endless task of finding something that makes them feel worthy. If the Storyteller can no longer sustain the ego financially and does not accept this reality, they are at risk to slipping back to Victim level.

How to heal the Control Freak.

To heal the Control Freak, you must come to the realization that **you have no control over anything but your thoughts and actions.** Believing you have any control over your life means you have identified with the world you have created in your mind. Unless the Control Freak recognizes their behavior is the exact behavior they are trying to avoid, they ultimately run out of people and situations to control and end up alone and isolated.

Both the Storyteller and Control Freak come from the Victim's low self-esteem; it has a devastating effect on their self-worth.

Low self-esteem is created when you believe what other people think and say about you or you fabricate what you want to be true about yourself. If your upbringing included negative criticism, disapproving attitudes, or a belief system where you suffer consequences for your actions, these behaviors can manifest into self-loathing, shame, and guilt.

Self-esteem vs. Self-worth.

Self-esteem is an integral part of our personal happiness, including the need to have fulfilling relationships and achieving dreams and desires. However, self-esteem is derived by what we think about ourselves and how we believe others perceive us.

Self-worth is an internal state of being that is attained through self-love, self-acceptance, and self-respect.

"Sometimes the hardest part of the journey is believing you're worth the trip."

Glenn Beck, Radio Host

"No magic potions.
No fairy dust.
No one will do it for you.
Just me,
I will push you,
show you,
how to put one determined
foot in front of the other.
That's what I will do.
I'm inside you.
I'm called your
Inner strength.
Dig down deep
and find me."

Author unknown

JOURNAL

Defining you—write as many answers as you can, regardless of how random. If you do not know, do not answer. Simply move on and do not judge yourself. Come back to the question(s) when you can answer with certainty.

1. What makes you happy? What makes you *literally* laugh out loud?

   _____

   _____

   _____

   _____

2. What makes you sad? What makes you cry?

   _____

   _____

   _____

   _____

3. What makes you angry? What makes you lose control?

   _____

   _____

   _____

   _____

4. What are you afraid of? What do you lose sleep over?

_____

_____

_____

_____

5. What empowers you? What makes you feel like you can accomplish anything?

_____

_____

_____

_____

Until the Storyteller realizes they are attempting to live a life that does not exist and if the Control Freak continually seeks victims to control as a way emotionally anesthetize, they will never achieve any inner peace. **All their suffering is due to their beliefs, which have created their reality.** Yet they think they can find happiness by changing external circumstances to create the feelings they want to experience. This gives Storytellers and Control Freaks an immense sense of personal power when in fact it's nothing but ego. Unfortunately, most people do not make it past Level Two. **Your level of awareness is reflected by the choices you make, and those choices are based on how you view yourself.** The elevation to Level Three comes when you trust yourself enough to be your own guiding light.

"Your value doesn't decrease based on someone's inability to see your worth."

Unknown

When the Storyteller tires of their own charade and the Control Freak sits alone in isolation; a thought might occur that something must change might occur to them, or not. This is the turning point where they make the choice to remain at Level Two because it is manageable, drop back to Level One because it is familiar, or listen to their soul calling them to seek change - a knowing that there is more to life beyond their current existence. Being brave enough to listen and courageous enough to follow elevates the Storyteller to the You Turn.

Life is all about choices, and it is time to make a choice. **It is time to take responsibility for who you are and what you have allowed yourself to become.** Start by letting go of your past because it no longer defines you. Stop focusing on your future because you have no power over it.

Level Three consciousness is about healing your past and loving yourself right now, **discovering what an amazing and beautiful person you are, just as you are.** As you shift your perception to seeing your flaws as what makes you unique and not an opportunity to self-criticize, you stop judging other people. You no longer care what other people think of you because your voice is the only one that matters. This is a shift to the Higher Self, **an inner calling from your Soul.**

"Attachment to things drops away by itself when you no longer seek to find yourself in them."

Eckhart Tolle

Centering Thought

I release the Storyteller because I am no longer concerned about the opinions of other people. I release the Control Freak, knowing it was a manifestation of my unresolved pain. Today I resign myself from being the narrator of my self-delusion. Embracing my authenticity, I am committed to finding out who I truly am and accepting that I am loving a divine creation. As I discover the beauty in myself, I shall seek to find the beauty in others and all that surrounds me.

Daily Affirmation

I am not concerned with how others see me.
I am defined by how I see myself.

"STOP LOOKING OUTSIDE YOURSELF FOR HELP. YOU'RE SOURCED AND FUELLED AND FUNDED BY A RENEWABLE RESOURCE, *which is within you.* IT NEVER RUNS OUT. IT IS YOUR ESSENCE. IT'S YOUR LIFE."

REVEREND MICHAEL BERNARD BECKWITH
SPIRITUAL LEADER AND AUTHOR

Journal

Journal

Level Three

THE YOU TURN

We've hit a fork on the path. It is time to make a choice. Your choices are taking personal responsibility and gaining control of your life or continuing to live as a Victim, a Storyteller, or a Control Freak. People who choose to live at the Victim and/or Storyteller level of awareness give their power away to others. Two of the main reason for this is part of them does not believe they can run their own lives, or they do not feel they are good enough just as they are. Both reasons are generated by self-perceptions.

Each time you handle life's situations, take responsibility for the outcome, no longer fear what happens or what others think — you become more empowered, self-reliant and connected to your Higher Self. As you develop trust in your choices and journey within for answers, you rely less on others and "group thought" to affect the direction of your life. **This creates the space for inner peace to exist.**

"Show me someone who is humble enough to accept and take responsibility for his or her circumstances and courageous enough to take whatever initiative is necessary to creatively work his or her way through or around these challenges, and I'll show you the supreme power of choice."

Stephen R. Covey,
American educator and author

The You Turn begins with personal accountability, your acknowledgment of past behavior, and becoming conscious of any current Victim, Storyteller and Control Freak mentality. Without judgment, start to mindfully shift repetitive thoughts and behaviors into conscious decisions and productive choices. This is done by directing your attention to something positive when you catch yourself ruminating over something negative. By working with the brain's neuroplasticity (your brain's ability to change and adapt) such as learning how to play an instrument or doing something creative, we generate new connections between the neurons in the brain. When we modify our thought pattern by doing different activities, we can restructure the brain's default mode of operation. Understanding how our brains function gives us the ability to shift from reliving a negative experience to creating a new one.

Dopamine, the neurotransmitter that effects mood and pleasure, as well as the "motivation, reward and reinforcement cycle", is released any time the brain expects to be rewarded. Fueled by anticipation, your brain does not know if you are learning something new or buying something new because the chemical response is the same. Redirecting your thoughts and actions creates new connections and pathways while weakening old thought patterns and programmed responses. With consistency, a positive outlook and practicing mindfulness such as being present, your brain will adapt to a new mindset.

To some extent, each of us have been Victims of our past, but it is how much of that past we allow to affect our present that will determine our future level of happiness. When you decide to no longer blame anyone or anything, including yourself, you get the opportunity to experience who you truly are. Your looks, talents, and what you perceive as flaws and imperfections not only make you individual-they are what make you remarkable in this vast universe. **There never has been nor will there ever be another you.** Think about that for a moment. **You are a miracle, because you came from a miracle. To refer to yourself as a miracle is your birthright.**

" A bird sitting in a tree
is never afraid of the branch
breaking,
because the trust is not in the
branch
but its ability
to fly."

Author unknown

Back to making choices. You can continue to live like a Victim, Storyteller, or Control Freak like a bird waiting for the next branch to break (and it will—they are supposed to break) or see yourself as a powerful expression of divinity, able to achieve and worthy of inner peace; and then you will learn how to fly.

The first two levels of consciousness are about being afraid of taking control of your life which is why the Victim and Storyteller give their power away to other people. That fear can come from not knowing who they are, not trusting their own ability to make good choices, not being able to learn from past mistakes, and the inability process consequences. Creating a reality that you want others to believe is yours or following influencers and celebrities on social media provides the perfect distraction from making the You Turn. This behavior, the attempt is to live a life that does not exist or by living vicariously through other people, causes you lose your identity, your individuality, and the desire to seek what makes **YOU** happy. Level Three is about knowing yourself well enough to make conscious choices that are for your highest good, your spiritual growth, and individual enlightenment.

EXERCISE

Defining yourself. Respond by giving as many answers as you can. If you do not know the answer, skip it. Feel free to write a statement about yourself when you are certain of how you feel.

1. What makes me cool, unique?

   _____

   _____

2. What makes me weird, different?

   _____

_____

3. What do I want to never change about me?

_____

_____

4. What has changed the most about me?

_____

_____

5. Compliments I have received.

_____

_____

6. What is the nicest thing anyone has ever done for me?

_____

_____

7. Criticisms I have received.

_____

_____

8. What is the worst thing anyone ever did to me?

_____

_____

9. Best day(s) ever.

_____

_____

10. Worst day(s) ever.

_____

_____

> "Not forgiving is like drinking rat poison and waiting for the rat to die."
>
> Anne Lamott, American novelist

Forgiveness is essential to regaining personal power and developing trust in yourself. The lack of forgiveness keeps us at Level One, the Victim, because it tethers us to the past preventing any inner healing to occur. When we harbor resentment, anger, hatred, and regret, we give the memory or person the power to make us feel those hidden emotions. **Forgiveness is in no way justification or condonation for wrongdoing.** Although forgiveness appears to be a weak response to a conflict, **it takes tremendous moral integrity to forgive. And the most difficult person to forgive is yourself.**

When is time to forgive?

- When you feel hatred in your heart.
- When your emotional fuse is short, and anger arises quickly.
- When you realize you have given someone else the power to steal your peace and rob you of your joy.

- When you ruminate and allow negative thoughts and bad memories to consume a good portion of your day.
- When you keep reliving a conversation or event that happened a while ago and you still become emotional or upset.
- When you experience sleepless nights and physical aches and pains especially in the chest.
- When you start wishing bad things on someone or certain people.
- When you are no longer comfortable with who you are. This one might be being called to be a higher version of yourself.

How to forgive.

- Acknowledge the emotional drain and waste of time not forgiving yourself or someone else is having on your life.
- Want to forgive. Question what you are holding on to by not forgiving.
- Be willing to give up being right for doing what is right.
- Understand and accept that everyone behaves at their level of awareness. Lower expectations and eliminate judgements.
- Accept people as they are. Find common ground and how you can grow from every relationship – especially the difficult ones.
- Believe everyone is trying their best. Everyone is going through something. EVERYONE.
- Increase your ability to forgive the little things. Then the big things, the things you thought were impossible to forgive, especially the ability to forgive yourself, ignites a powerful healing process within and frees the soul.
- You contribute to vast, universe and expressing the powerful energy of forgiveness, raises and heals collective consciousness of our planet as well as our universe.

Why forgive?

- To regain power over your life.
- To set you free from the past.
- To change your inner voice.
- To give yourself permission to move on.
- To increase your self-worth, inner strength, and integrity.
- To develop the ability to rise above emotions and toxic situations.
- To maintain health, mental wellness, and peace of mind.
- To build character and learn from a great teacher—YOU!
- To honor the Divine in you.

Forgiving is difficult, impossible at times, because it is perceived as giving in and leaves you vulnerable to criticism. That is why people find it so difficult. However, not forgiving has been linked to depression, anxiety, hostility, and substance abuse. Ironically, the one who suffers these ills is the one unwilling to forgive.

Forgiveness requires tremendous emotional strength and spiritual courage. It lowers blood pressure, improves heart health, increases self-esteem, builds up all immune systems, and fosters understanding, compassion, and healthier relationships. Most importantly, forgiveness frees you from your past.

"True forgiveness is when you can say Thank you for that experience."

Oprah Winfrey, American talk show host

EXERCISE

Forgiving others. Think about the challenging relationships in your life and the people you need to forgive. Respond to the questions:

1. What do you know about the person you need to forgive? Specifically, who raised them and how they were raised?

_____

_____

2. Write down any thoughts or stories they may have told you that might give insight into their upbringing.

_____

_____

3. Based on the first three levels of this book, do you believe that they have Victim, Storyteller or Control Freak behavior? Which ones? Have they made the You turn and taken responsibility for their choices and actions? Be specific.

_____

_____

4. Do see any connection between how they behave as adults and their upbringing?

_____

_____

5. From a place of empathy, can you sense any of their emotional wounds? Can you understand how these feelings were created?

_____

_____

6. Do you need to forgive this person in order to set yourself free from the emotional control you have given them?

_____

_____

_____

_____

_____

7. What would that take?

_____

_____

_____

_____

8. How would that feel?

_____

_____

_____

_____

_____

Taking responsibility or being accountable is not about shame, blame, or guilt. It is about acknowledging that you have the power to influence the events and circumstances of your life. You navigated the direction of your life so far; because you survived all the trials and tribulations, you have experienced your inner strength and determination. Level Three is the shift from co-dependency to self-reliance, regaining trust in yourself and building self-worth. To help define what self-worth is, let us determine what it is not.

Self-worth is NOT determined by:

- How much money or how many things you have.
- Your relationship status.
- Your social media following.
- Your title, position, and the amount of your income.
- The level of education you have achieved.
- The number of friends you have.
- Your appearance or age.
- What other people think.

"Forgive those who didn't know how to treat you. They were teaching you how to love yourself."

Ryan Elliot

" SELF-WORTH:

THE ABILITY TO COMPREHEND
AND ACCEPT MY TRUE
VALUE—
TO UNDERSTAND I AM MORE
THAN MY MIND, BODY,
EMOTIONS AND BEHAVIORS,
TO SEE ME AS GOD SEES
ME, TO ACCEPT HIS LOVE FOR
ME AND TO LOVE MYSELF IN
A LIKE MANNER."

DR. CHRISTINA HIBBERT, CLINICAL PSYCHOLOGIST.

You determine your self-worth by what you believe to be true. Self-worth is deep inner awareness of who you are, your intrinsic purpose, and knowing that you are a part of something bigger than anything you think or believe about yourself. **You are necessary, irreplaceable, and are of immeasurable worth.** These are the words of the Soul which can only be heard when you silence the mind.

EXERCISE

Rate what you believe from 0 (not at all) to 10 (completely).

1. I am not afraid to make mistakes. _____
2. Even when people criticize me, I can handle it. _____
3. Generally speaking, I like the way I look. _____
4. Even when others reject me, I love myself. _____
5. I am successful at solving problems. _____
6. I am proud of my accomplishments. _____
7. I feel worthy of respect. _____
8. I would rather be me than anyone else. _____
9. I love to try new things. _____
10. I believe in me. _____
11. I focus on my accomplishments, not my failures. _____
12. When I receive a compliment, it increases my feeling of wellbeing and not my ego. _____
13. I feel best when I am at the service of others. _____
14. I genuinely love who I am. _____
15. I rarely compare myself with others. _____

The least you can score is 0 points, and the most you can score is 150 points. Rate where you are to get a general idea how you feel about yourself. Focus on the low scores and find solutions to increase your self-worth and decrease the voice of the inner critic.

"Self-love. Self-respect. Self-worth:
There's a reason they all start with 'self.'
You can't find them in anyone else."

Unknown

Each level of this journey highlights a different state of consciousness; once acknowledged, that awareness becomes a choice. Your level of consciousness increases as you move past the challenges each level presents. **Level Three invites you to be the creator of your destiny and walk in the direction of your dreams.**

Creating boundaries and a new mindset are needed to move forward on your journey. Be warned, the path to inner peace is solo and living by a higher standard of accountability will disconnect you from people who do not have the interest, desire or ability to raise their level of consciousness.

JOURNAL

A New Mindset. Write about how you will respond and handle each of the changes below:

1. How will you be mindful of your inner voice and consciously replace negative statements with positive affirmations that you believe about yourself?

_____

_____

_____

_____

2. Your people-pleasing days are over, and your needs come first. What changes must be made to focus the attention on *you.*

_____

_____

_____

_____

3. Your value comes from within, and you set the standard. From most to least, what is important to you?

_____

_____

_____

_____

4. Other people's opinions and judgments must be scrutinized. You have the power to rise above all criticism because your self-worth is determined by you and no one else. What steps will you take to be more conscious of what people are saying? How will you handle criticism constructively?

_____

_____

_____

_____

5. No more focusing on other people—it's time to find out who you are, what you're capable of, and what your purpose is. What effort will you make to find your unique gifts and talents?

_____

_____

_____

_____

6. No more worrying about the future or thinking about the past. What actions can you take to stop yourself from worrying or ruminating?

_____

_____

_____

7. Every day, regardless of what happens, you have the resources, both internal and external, to handle anything life throws at you. You have survived this far, which reflects your true nature and is a testament to your capabilities and strength. What actions can you take to shift your mindset to reveal the capable person that you are?

_____

_____

_____

_____

8. Although you have no power over your feelings you are responsible for controlling your emotions. What actions can you take to maintain a positive state of mind?

_____

_____

_____

_____

9. Write yourself a love letter. Use your first name. Read it to yourself in the mirror. Don't forget to glance up and look yourself in the eyes.

_____

_____

_____

10. Make quiet time and reflect on the person you want to become. Align with your Higher Self. When will you make the time for stillness?

_____

_____

_____

_____

_____

Power Points by Louise Hay:
"I believe in my own power to change."

1. We are each responsible for our own experiences.
2. Every thought we think is creating our own future.
3. Everyone is dealing with the damaging patterns of resentment, criticism, guilt, and self-hatred.
4. There are only thoughts and thoughts can be changed.
5. We need to release and forgive everyone.
6. Self-approval and self-acceptance are in the "now" and are the keys to positive change.
7. The point of power is in the present moment.

Louise Hay Author and spiritual healer

Centering Thought

Today I have the strength of self-empowerment through forgiveness. I emotionally detach from the expectations of others that used to define me as I now have the courage to forgive all who have hurt me including myself. By releasing my anger and frustration I can begin to bring light to my soften heart and trust myself as the master of my fate.

Daily Affirmation

I am complete.
I am beautiful.
I am worthy.

Journal

_____

_____

_____

_____

_____

_____

_____

_____

_____

_____

_____

_____

_____

_____

_____

_____

_____

_____

Journal

Journal

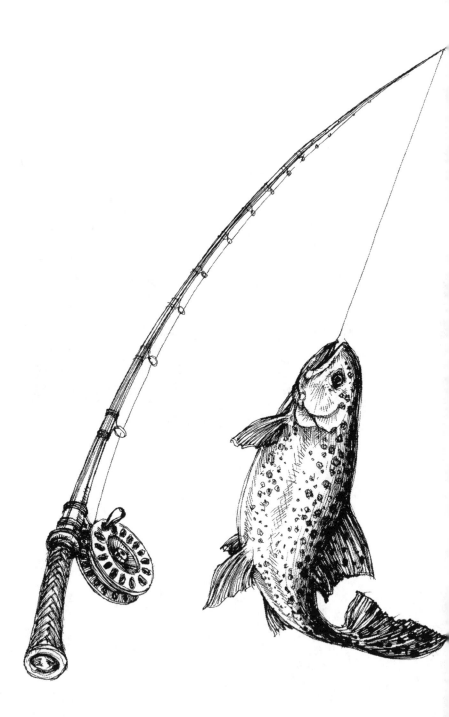

Level Four

LIFE HAPPENS FOR YOU

Life can provide an experience or an unexpected event that makes you question everything you thought was true. The unconscious mind will see life as a series of problems, victim mentality. The conscious mind will see them as challenges and find empowerment by facing and resolving life's inevitable hardships. This simple shift of perspective is the foundation of Level Four: Life Happens FOR You.

Nothing on this planet is exempt from facing challenges: not animals, birds, insects, or plants. **Challenges increase your chances of survival; that is their purpose**. Think of a palm tree and what it takes to endure during a storm. With each torrential wind that blows, it bends further and grows more resilient so it can tolerate a hurricane or a typhoon. Avoiding, ignoring, or blaming others for your problems keeps you a victim of circumstances. Each challenge you overcome builds self-reliance, resiliency, and coping skills so when your storm comes, you will have strength to weather it. **Accepting life's challenges, rather than resisting them, is essential to achieving a Level Four consciousness.**

The Power of Challenges.

- Challenges help define priorities, what is important, and what you value.
- Challenges bond you to everybody on the planet. They level the human playing field. Everyone everywhere experiences challenges.
- They give us the opportunity to share emotions, work together, and support each other.
- Challenges make you humble. Humility keeps you from being arrogant, pretentious, egotistic, and conceited.
- Nothing sparks creativity and is more rewarding than finding a solution to a challenge.
- Challenges with solution-based results end drama, complaining, and enabling.
- If you are facing challenges, it means you are alive. This alone should make you happy!

"Challenges are what make life interesting. Conquering them is what makes life meaningful."

Joshua J. Marine, author, and magician

How to deal with challenges

- Acknowledgment
- Devise solutions
- Execution
- Reflection

If any of these steps are missing from the process, the challenge will persist and manifest into a reoccurring problem. **There is tremendous spiritual growth when we confront, face, and resolve**

our hardships. The fact that human experience includes surviving devastation, destruction and tragedy indicates we are *well* equipped to rise above, to heal and transform through adversity.

Challenge Checklist

1. Define what the challenge is and understand it.
2. Find creative ways to solve it without worrying about the outcome.
3. Take action! No more talking about what you're going to do.
4. Assess the progress. What is working and what is not? Draw a conclusion.
5. Commit to a resolution and learn from the experience so it ends, and you can move on.

EXERCISE

Using the format above, list a challenge you are facing right now. Put this plan into action and resolve one of your challenges.

Challenge:

_____

_____

_____

_____

Possible solution(s):

_____

_____

_____

_____

Possible obstacles:

_____

_____

_____

_____

Plan of action:

_____

_____

_____

_____

Assessment/Review: What's going right? What's going wrong? What needs to change?

_____

_____

_____

Resolution:

_____

_____

_____

_____

Conclusion/Reflection:

_____

_____

_____

_____

> *"Take the opportunity to learn from your mistakes: find the cause of your problem and eliminate it. Don't try to be perfect; just be an excellent example of being human."*

Tony Robbins, author, and Life Coach

Level Four is about how you respond to life's inevitable changes and challenging relationships. **Your trials and tribulations are not designed to take you down but rather are a way to connect with, trust, and rely on yourself.** They are an opportunity to examine the struggles within, refocus your attention, and define what is important in your life.

The Tale of Two Wolves

One evening, an elder Cherokee brave told his grandson about a battle that goes on inside people. He said "my son the battle is between two 'wolves' inside us all. One is evil. It is anger, envy, jealousy, regret, greed, arrogance, inferiority, lies, false-pride, superiority and ego.

The other is good. It is joy, peace, love, serenity, humility, kindness, benevolence, empathy, generosity, truth, compassion and faith."

The grandson thought about it for a minute and asked his grandfather, "Which one wins?"

The old Cherokee simply replied, "The one you feed."

(Nanticokeindians.org)

The grandfather states there are two wolves within, one being evil and one being good, and it highlights our human struggles with inner duality. Level Four consciousness acknowledges both exist and the need to find balance between them. The "evil" wolf is afraid, howling for your attention, signaling something within you is unresolved. **As you tackle each challenge you build faith in yourself, lessening the fear of any outcome.** This allows you to shift focus to feeding the "good" wolf and achieving the joyful life you deserve. **The more personal responsibility you take over the challenges in your life, the more resilient to adverse situations you become.**

"A crisis creates the opportunity to dig deep into the reservoirs of our very being, to rise to the levels of confidence, strength, and resolve we otherwise didn't think we possessed. Through adversity, we come face to face who we really are and what really counts."

Jon Huntsman Jr.
American businessman and philanthropist

Perceptions vs. Reality.

Our sensory receptors (sight, sound, taste, and touch) receive and process external information constantly so we can interact with our environment. Through the process of collecting and organizing, we interpret this information, creating perceptions. **Perceptions are not reality**. Perceptions are how we view the world based on many things such as past experiences, emotions, needs, values, prejudices, and expectations. Because of the vast ingredients that make up perceptions, it stands to reason that each person will not see the same thing the same way. Seeing a glass half full or half empty is an example of this phenomenon. Our perceptions influence our decisions, choices, beliefs, and actions based on what we believe is real. The more we know ourselves, our strengths and limitations, the more we can align with the truth, what is reality.

"Everything we hear is an opinion, not fact. Everything we see is perspective, not truth."

Marcus Aurelius

The Reality of Perception.

- Question and challenge your perceptions. They might not be real, just your current reality.
- Be open to other people's perceptions. They might be right and offer a fresh and different perspective.
- Be flexible with your perceptions. They may no longer serve you well and need adjusting as your consciousness grows.
- Be mindful that you might distort the truth to suit your perception. Lying to yourself about your reality is victim mentality.

Becoming conscious of how you perceive your reality benefits you in two ways — first, by understanding you might be creating a problem when none exist — and second, that each person can see the same situation from a completely different perspective. This expansion of awareness allows you to be more inclusive and open when dealing with challenging people and difficult circumstances.

"Being challenged in life is inevitable.
Being defeated is optional."

Rodger Crawford, Hall of Fame athlete, motivational speaker

Awareness of your perceptions allows you to see where you can be more conscious and less judgmental. Pick one of your perspectives and try to see it from the opposite side. For example, if seeing someone in a wheelchair makes you feel uncomfortable, experience sitting in one and feel what it is like to be that person. Seeing the world from someone else's viewpoint opens your heart to compassion and empathy rather than pity and sympathy.

When you consider each person has a unique perception of life based on a litany of circumstances, it is understandable that these differences can cause conflicts in relationships. Shared experiences, such as a being raised by two working parents, could result in opposite future choices by siblings put in the same situation. Every experience is individual, creates an opinion, and that opinion creates an expectation. Expectations are based on beliefs. If you do not know what you believe, need, want, or expect from relationships, you will continually attempt to change people to fulfill whatever it is you are lacking. No one has the responsibility to make you happy except you. Control Freak behavior — believing you can change someone, empowers the ego's sense of superiority, ignites false control, and usually ends the relationship. Your ego will never hold you accountable for the failure of any relationship and will continue to seek similar relationships because they are familiar, and that choice will guarantee a repeat experience. If your happiness is reliant on people or being needed by people, it will be unsustainable as life situations change ending with disappointment and even heartbreak. Like things, people are external and being with certain people brings you happiness, the reality is, **no one has the ability to make you truly happy.**

"Expectation is the root of all heartache."

Unknown

By defining what you need and want helps you focus on connecting with people that want the same things. Any unprocessed emotions, repressed feelings, hurt or anger follows you like a shadow until you shed light on them. Acknowledging and healing residual emotions is the opportunity for self-reflection and personal growth so you can bring the best version of yourself into every relationship.

JOURNAL

Define relationships. Answer the questions with as many responses as possible.

1. What are the most important things in a relationship?

_____

_____

_____

_____

_____

_____

2. What are unimportant things in a relationship?

_____

_____

_____

3. What have I learned about myself from past relationships?

_____

_____

_____

_____

4. What mistakes am I responsible for in past relationships?

_____

_____

_____

_____

5. How have I corrected those mistakes?

_____

_____

_____

6. What am I willing to change for someone else?

_____

_____

_____

_____

7. What am I unwilling to change for someone?

_____

_____

_____

_____

8. What do I expect from a relationship?

_____

_____

_____

9. What will make me walk away from a relationship?

_____

_____

_____

10. What will make me stay in a relationship?

_____

_____

_____

_____

When we interpret other people's thoughts, words, or actions through our self-created belief system, our perceptions can distort reality. If we continue to see life through a finite perspective, we restrict understanding others as well as ourselves. As your awareness elevates, you will begin to see people operating at different levels of consciousness giving you a better understanding of their mindset, reasoning and behavior.

As with all relationships, the only power you have is how you respond to them. The less you define people by your opinions and criticism the more you will see the unique beauty that lies within everyone you encounter.

How to deal with difficult people and challenging relationships.

- Begin to recognize the physical response you have to certain people and stay calm. Pause and take a few breaths any time you feel tension within your body. Monitor your feelings and take a moment and regain control. Don't allow your emotions to elevate to theirs. Difficult people use emotional responses to control a relationship or situation.
- Overcome the fear of conflict. Not every interaction has to turn into a fight with challenging people. All relationships require negotiation. Learn how to communicate your feelings effectively and defend what you believe.
- Establish boundaries. You teach people how to treat you by accepting their behavior and allowing it to continue. Being

the recipient of a psychological projection (when someone transfers negative feelings about themselves on to you rather than dealing with the internal conflict within themselves) you relinquish your power to them. Sometimes ignoring or avoiding difficult people is the best way to protect your peace. Walking away or ending relationships might be the only solution in order to move forward.

- Listen attentively and respond with integrity and civility. Apply the Golden Rule and treat others as you wish to be treated regardless of how they are treating you. This will help diffuse conflicts and elevates the conversation to a higher, more mature level.

- Difficult people are difficult for a reason. Whether you feel compelled to find out the motivation for their behavior or not, the best response to difficult people is with compassion. The wall they build around themselves keeps them trapped in misery and emotionally isolated. Practicing empathy is beneficial for the rewiring of your brain to develop a resiliency for challenging relationships.

- Be mindful that you are not unconsciously provoking challenging people. A mocking smile, a condescending tone or aggressive body language can send an unintended message.

- Avoid arguing and discussing conflicting or trigger topics while interacting with people you find difficult to be around. Listen to your gut when you sense things are about to go bad. Have an exit plan. Excuse yourself from the situation.

- Acknowledge your ability to rise above! It takes a lot of energy to control the natural human response to attack when you feel your being attacked, belittled, or threatened. Talk the experience through with someone you trust. Let off any residual emotions through physical activity such as walking.

To rise above challenges, you must hold yourself to a higher standard of behavior and be accountable for your actions. To focus on goodwill, self-discipline, truth, and integrity shifts perceptions and creates a virtuous existence. Remember the aspects of the good wolf? Joy, peace, love, hope, serenity, humility, kindness, benevolence, generosity, truth, compassion, and faith. **A shift of your attention will dramatically enhance the quality of your life**. Choosing to live a virtuous life will impact the direction of your moral compass, your character as well as your values.

> "It's the one thing you can control. You are responsible for how people remember you – or don't. So don't take it lightly."

Kobe Bryant, Professional basketball player

Published on October 22, 1925, in *"Young Indian"*, lawyer, spiritual leader and activist, Mahatma Gandhi, wrote about the seven things that will destroy humanity. Take note how each "sin" is social condition, and the "antidote" is a high moral standard. It has been almost 100 years since the publishing of this article, and this concept is as relevant today as it was a century ago.

Mahatma Gandhi speaks of the Seven Social Sins.

- Wealth without work.
- Pleasure without conscience.
- Knowledge without character.
- Business without ethics.
- Science without humanity.
- Religion without sacrifice.
- Politics without principle.

JOURNAL

Using the Seven Social Sins, make statements out of each. For example, number one, attaining wealth without work might make someone not appreciate what they have, not understand the power and value of money; and never realize their true potential.

As we accept life's challenges as opportunities for self-reliance and a way to build resilience to adversity, we move forward to Level Five where Life Happens Through You: and begin to address the emotional aspects of being human.

- _____
- _____
- _____
- _____
- _____
- _____
- _____

"Don't be distracted by criticism. Remember—the only taste of success some people have is when they take a bite out of you."

Zig Ziglar, author, salesman and motivational speaker

Centering Thought

My sheer existence is proof I have never been given more than I can handle. The challenges I have faced were an invitation to increase my fortitude, realize my potential, and discover my inner strength. I thank the universe for showing me answers to every problem during my life's journey.

Daily Affirmation

Today, I will face challenges with a sense of adventure! When I focus my attention on creative solutions, they will appear. I know the answers to all my problems lie within me and that I can rise above anything.

Journal

Journal

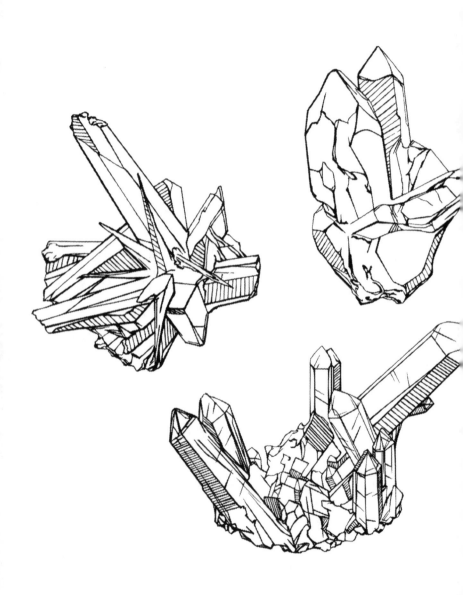

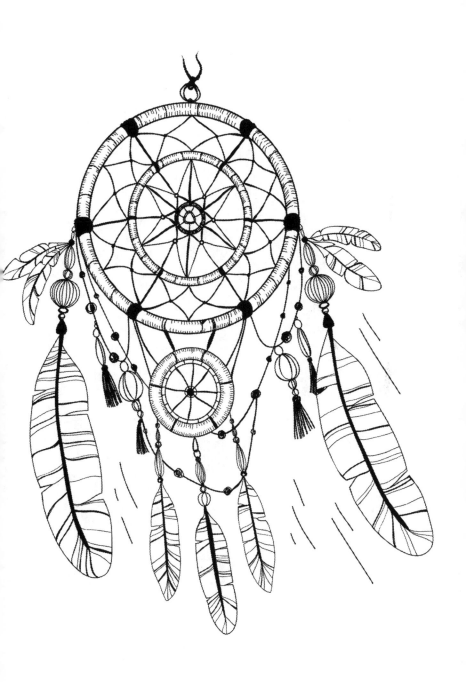

Level Five

LIFE HAPPENS THROUGH YOU

Level Four explains how the trial and tribulations of life are not designed to destroy our spirit but are intended to elevate our consciousness – by accepting that each challenge we overcome fosters inner strength; and builds trust that the universe has our best interests at heart, with many important lessons to teach us. To think any other way will hinder alignment with Source.

Life events, especially traumatic ones, can leave us with unexpected, unwanted, and unresolved emotions. **Being human, we have no control over our emotional reactions, or the part of the brain processes them,** nor can we choose our feelings, even though they drive our actions and decisions. **Level Five consciousness is taking responsibility for your emotions and allowing them to flow through you.**

"This being human is a guesthouse.
Every morning a new arrival.
A joy, a depression, a meanness,
some momentary awareness
comes
as an unexpected visitor.
Welcome and entertain them all!
Even if they're a crowd of
sorrows,
who violently sweep your house
of its furniture,
still, treat each one honorably.
He might be clearing you out for
some new delight.
The dark thought, the shame,
the malice, meet them at the door
laughing, and invite them in.
Be grateful for whoever comes,
for each has been sent as a guide
from beyond."

Jalaluddin Rumi, 13th-century Persian poet

Facts About Feelings.

- There are no moral ethics to your feelings. They are not right, wrong, good, bad—they just are.
- Emotions can be repressed, but that does not make them go away.
- Feelings can lead you to make both good and bad choices.
- The more you ignore an emotion, the more you empower it.
- The only way to address an emotion is to feel it.
- Your feelings direct your thoughts, but you can use those same thoughts to manage your feelings.
- The only power you have over your feelings is how you handle them.

"I don't want to be at the mercy of my emotions. I want to use them, enjoy them and dominate them."

Oscar Wilde, Irish poet

Feelings are the reaction to an emotional state of being. Becoming aware and able to identify what you are feeling lessens their intensity. This gives you the opportunity to vocalize and express your emotions, allowing them to move through you rather than build up within or define you.

Intense emotions can be an indication that something needs your attention or has been repressed. We know emotions cannot be rationalized or justified, but they can cause tremendous internal suffering if left unaddressed. This internal suffering can potentially change someone as they ruminate on negative thoughts that integrate into their personalities. Someone who starts out being angry at a life situation can become a miserable person by the repetitious thoughts "firing and wiring" together in their brain. Rather than feel the emotion, they become the emotion. Once people become an emotion, it often manifests into a mental and/or physical illness.

How we handle our emotions is the only power we have over them. The space created in Level One that allows thoughts to flow through is the same pathway that allows emotions to arise. You are "here", and the emotion is "there". When you are the observer, and access Soul consciousness, you allow feelings to "be" without any judgment. In this space feeling can be traced back to their source.

JOURNAL

Write responses to the following questions:

1. Are you aware of your emotions as the arise?

_____

_____

_____

_____

2. Do you suppress feelings to avoid a confrontation?

_____

_____

_____

_____

3. Do you acknowledge and allow yourself to feel all emotions?

_____

_____

_____

_____

_____

4. Do you block any emotions? Which ones? Why do you think that is?

_____

_____

_____

_____

_____

5. Do you prefer to write or verbally express how you feel?

_____

_____

_____

_____

_____

6. Are you effective in expressing your emotions to other people? What specific ways can you improve your communication skills?

_____

_____

_____

_____

7. Have your emotions ever made you feel physically ill? When? What thoughts trigger that reaction?

_____

_____

_____

_____

8. Have you ever felt your feelings do not matter? In what circumstances?

_____

_____

_____

_____

_____

9. What would have to change to empower you to rise above your emotions?

_____

_____

_____

_____

_____

_____

As you become mindful of your emotions and what might trigger them, you can learn different techniques to calm emotions, such as breathwork, and develop ways to express yourself peacefully and effectively.

> "Between stimulus and response there is a space. In that space there is a power to choose a response. In our response lies our growth and our freedom."

Victor Frankl, Austrian neurologist, psychiatrist, philosopher, author and Holocaust survivor

When we are faced with an unexpected setback or negative situation, taking a moment to pause helps reset our brains. The human brain and different systems throughout our body affect our emotions. The more we understand how our brains interpret each situation we face, the more we can self-regulate our response.

"SELF-CONTROL
IS STRENGTH.
CALMNESS IS MASTERY.

YOU HAVE TO GET TO THE POINT WHERE
YOUR MOOD DOESN`T SHIFT BASED
ON THE INSIGNIFICANT ACTIONS
OF SOMEONE ELSE.
DON`T ALLOW OTHERS
TO CONTROL THE
THE DIRECTION
OF YOUR LIFE.
DON`T ALLOW YOUR EMOTIONS
TO OVERPOWER
YOUR INTELLIGENCE."

MORGAN FREEMAN, AMERICAN ACTOR

The autonomic nervous system, like many other systems in the body, works without our conscious effort, which is why we need to become conscious of it. This system has two primary parts: the sympathetic and parasympathetic. Both react to external information are designed for basic survival. While we rarely experience a truly physically threatening situation, a perception of fear can trigger the autonomic nervous system which impacts our feelings as well as our reality.

Using the good wolf and evil wolf analogy, the evil wolf, a.k.a. the sympathetic nervous system, has the task of warning you of a dangerous situation. A flood of hormones prepares your body for "fight, flight, or to freeze" as shoulders rise, heart rate and alertness increase in response to a perceived threat. The good wolf, the parasympathetic system, restores the body to a calm state by releasing a counter hormone when you breathe and calm your mind. Because the evil wolf is the "protector," he reacts first, and the hormones epinephrine, cortisol, and adrenaline are released, causing an intense physical reaction. It takes time for the body to regain composure even after the body releases the good wolf hormones (acetylcholine, dopamine and serotonin), which is why taking a moment is the appropriate response to an inflamed situation.

If you were experiencing a dangerous situation right now, your body would have a physical reaction before your mind realized what was going on. Although your body can protect you from perceived danger, it is your thoughts that determine what that danger is.

Reacting and Responding.

Every day, your emotions wax and wane based on visual stimuli, daily challenges, and emotional reactions. As we process these events, we react in accordance with our belief system, our level of understanding and temperament. Because our emotions are primal and uncontrollable, they can result in physical, unconscious, and regrettable actions.

A reaction is a compulsive act without consideration of any consequences. As an event escalates, the "fight or flight" hormones get released into the bloodstream, making a person aggressive and confrontational. This usually ends up with a counterattack and no resolution. Think of road rage.

A response requires a pause and consciousness, and it allows for hormones to subside. From there you can be assertive without aggression. Clear, nonemotionally actions can be taken and an amicable resolution can be achieved. **When you react to a person, they are in control. When you respond to a person, you are in control.**

A fast-paced, stressful lifestyle will force the adrenal glands to remain in a constant state of fight or flight, waiting for the next attack. Because the body is not designed to be exposed to consistently high levels of stress hormones, it wreaks havoc on our health by resulting in anxiety, depression, high blood pressure, and diabetes. **Since thoughts create our reality, if you change the way you think, you can literally change your life.**

Level Five consciousness invites you to acknowledge and feel all your emotions. **Restricting the flow of negative emotions restricts the flow of positive ones.** Once you are aware of your feelings, you have the choice of how to act and respond.

EXERCISE

Emotional empowerment. Should you find yourself in a situation that escalates into a confrontation, take a pause.

1. Is this issue important to me? Am I passionate enough to risk my emotional stability for this confrontation?

    _____

    _____

2. Am I focused on being right or doing what's right?

    _____

3. Is this person worth disrupting my peace? Is the relationship worth it?

_____

_____

_____

_____

4. What is the potential outcome? How will this encounter affect my future?

_____

_____

_____

_____

_____

5. What other actions can I take to resolve this issue other than confrontation?

_____

_____

_____

_____

_____

Emotions move through us when we acknowledge them, feel them, accept them, and let them go. The quicker we can process our emotions the less change they have of taking root, disrupting our inner peace, and stealing our joy. Knowing we have no power over our feelings, we surrender to the part of us that make us uniquely human and rely on our higher self – our Soul. Our Soul, our spiritual default system, has the resources to navigate human reactions that our rational minds do not understand as well as a response system that is out of our control. The mind will react. The Soul will respond.

How to allow emotions to move through you.

1. Acknowledge your feelings. Create a space for them to "be". You are "here" and the emotion is "there".
2. Feel your feelings but do not become them. Observe and question what your emotions are trying to tell you.
3. Understand emotions are part of the human condition and cannot be controlled but can be managed and worked through.
4. Accept whatever emotions come up. Do not judge or repress. Try to find the source or the cause of the feeling.
5. Realize that emotions fade, change, and end. Feelings do not last forever but can rob you of present moment awareness.
6. Shift and quiet negative emotions by doing something positive.
7. Give yourself permission to let go of any emotion that serves no purpose.
8. Smile. Replace negative thoughts with positive ones by envisioning a person or place that you love. Imagine breathing through your heart and allow your light to shine.

"I must not fear. Fear is a mind-killer. Fear is the little death that brings on total obliteration. I will face my fear. I will permit it to pass over me and through me. And when it has gone past, I will return the inner eye to see its path. Where the fear has gone, there will be nothing. Only I will remain."

Frank Herbert, science fiction writer.

"THERE ARE ONLY TWO EMOTIONS:

LOVE & FEAR.

ALL POSITIVE EMOTIONS COME FROM LOVE AND ALL NEGATIVE EMOTIONS COME FROM FEAR.

FROM LOVE FLOWS HAPPINESS, CONTENTMENT, PEACE & JOY.

FROM FEAR COMES ANGER, HATE, ANXIETY, AND GUILT.

IT'S TRUE THAT THERE ARE ONLY TWO PRIMARY EMOTIONS, LOVE & FEAR.

BUT IT'S MORE ACCURATE TO SAY THAT THERE IS ONLY LOVE OR FEAR, FOR WE CANNOT FEEL THESE TWO EMOTIONS TOGETHER, AT EXACTLY THE SAME TIME.

THEY'RE OPPOSITES.

IF WE'RE IN FEAR, WE'RE NOT IN A PLACE OF LOVE.

WHEN WE ARE IN A PLACE OF LOVE, WE CANNOT BE IN A PLACE OF FEAR."

ELISABETH KUBLER-ROSS, SWISS-AMERICAN PSYCHIATRIST

Love and Fear

Love and fear are the two core human emotions. Fear survives on lack and withdrawal and is generated from thoughts, opinions, and judgments. Love thrives on gratitude, inner peace, and contentment and is generated from within. When you figure out the source of your fear (usually from prejudice, ignorance, lack, trauma, perception, or collective group thought), you can better address the unconscious thoughts that feed that emotion.

Both love and fear release powerful hormones into our systems that cause us to react and prevent us from making rational decisions and choices. By simplifying all emotions into two categories, we can better address the root of all the other emotions we experience. The root of your anger over a situation might be the fear of the outcome. All negative emotions are derived from fear, so it is essential you examine the core of the emotion, face it, and work through to a resolution.

On to Level Six. Where you will begin to understand you are far greater than the version of yourself that you have created your current physical body. You are an expression of the universal energy that courses through everything, including your veins.

Level Six consciousness is about re-connecting to everyone and all that surrounds you. It is your thoughts and belief system that keep you separate from Oneness with the universe. Your divine purpose plays an important role in the collective energy of this planet and the next two levels invite you elevate your consciousness beyond its current limitations.

"Gravity explains the motions of the planets, but it cannot explain who put the planets in motion."

Sir Isaac Newton, English physicist

Centering Thought

Feelings are a part of the human experience and cannot be controlled. When I allow space for my emotions to arise, I can stand back and begin to recognize the parts of me that are seeking my attention and require healing. Rather than allowing feelings to hijack my peace, I become conscious of them, pause and take a breath, control my reaction, and express my feelings effectively from a place of love. When this becomes my natural state of being, I have aligned with my Higher Self, my Soul.

Daily Affirmation

Today, I will be aware of the feelings and emotions I experience during a 24-hour period. How they wax and wane between unconscious repetitive thoughts, exterior circumstances and what I pay attention to. Since I have the power to choose what my mind focuses on, I have complete control over whether I am happy or not. I have the freedom to make this choice every moment of every day. When I rise above the grip of my emotions, I can access universal love and connect with All That Is.

Journal

Journal

Journal

Level Six

LIFE IS YOU

If not for the explosion of stars that released the elements for evolution, you would not be here. Planetary scientist, Dr. Ashley King, of the Museum of Natural History in London explains, "It's totally true: nearly all the elements in the human body were made in a star and many have come through supernovas." **You are connected to everyone and everything. That is why you are important. That is why you matter to this planet.** Although you are currently housed within a physical body on planet Earth, you are born from an infinite universe and your essence is eternal.

> "We are all connected; to each other, biologically. To the earth, chemically. To the rest of the universe atomically."

Neil deGrasse Tyson, American Astrophysicist

The human body has approximately the same ratio of water as planet Earth: 70 percent. There is enough carbon in your body to make a diamond, you have the same genes as a head of lettuce and your brain is remarkably similar to the structure of the universe. Genomes, the instruction manual for all living things, tells an organism how to grow, build itself, and operate. After sequencing the entire genome sequences of various organisms, researchers have concluded all living creatures have some similar genetic machinery that is related to metabolism; and in this sense, find it is likely we came from one universal ancestor, concluding all things are related to one another.

As humans we share 99.9 percent of the same DNA as one another. No life on Earth shares that much. Within the 0.01 percent of DNA that gives us an individual appearance, there is not enough to create a different species of human. However, there is unique combination of DNA to makes you one of a kind. **You are an original expression of the Creator.**

The earth spins and the moon stabilizes its axis while the two miraculously dance in perfect gravitational harmony. Your body functions effortlessly, just as the universe does, with the innate knowledge of how to grow, operate, and heal. Consider your heart, the source of life, and how it beats without your conscious effort. Take a moment and consider who or what made that possible.

You must feed yourself, but you don't have to think about digestion. You need a good night's rest, but you don't have to be involved with the healing and repairing your body automatically does during sleep. You blink, breathe and swallow unconsciously all day long. There is an intelligence that is keeping you sustained without you knowing how it functions. God has given you the ability to survive without being consciously involved in the complex systems that keep you alive, giving you the power to choose and create your own life. Within you lies infinite knowledge. It is has always been there.

"The ego is not who you truly are. The ego is your self-image; your social mask: it is the role you are playing. Your social mask thrives on approval. It wants control, and it is sustained by power, because it lives in fear."

Deepak Chopra, Endocrinologist, author,
alternative-medicine advocate

Connectedness is the theme of Level Six. Knowing you are a part of an awe-inspiring universe is very empowering as a natural curiosity calls you to align with it. Focusing on where you fit, figuring out what you believe in, and finding your purpose ignites the Soul. However, certain thoughts and beliefs keep you from accessing your higher self: specifically, the ego.

The Soul and the Ego.

Your Soul is your essence, the light and immortal expression of the divine within you. The ego is a self-created version of you based on wants, needs, desires, and outside acceptance. Like the good and evil wolves, they are a part of who you are, and require balance. The one you feed will directly affect the level of your happiness.

The Ego vs. the Soul.

- The ego seeks to serve itself—the Soul seeks to **serve others.**
- The ego seeks outward recognition—the Soul seeks **inner authenticity.**
- The ego sees life as a competition—the Soul sees **life as a gift.**

- The ego seeks to self-preserve—the Soul seeks to **preserve others.**
- The ego looks outward—the Soul looks **inward.**
- The ego feels lack—the Soul feels **abundance.**
- The ego is mortal—the soul is **eternal.**
- The ego is drawn to lust—the soul is drawn to **love.**
- The ego seeks wisdom—the soul is **wisdom.**
- The ego enjoys the prize—the soul enjoys the **journey.**
- The ego is cause to pain—the soul is called to **healing.**
- The ego rejects God—the soul embraces **God.**
- The ego seeks to be filled—the Soul is eternal **wholeness.**
- The ego says "me"—the soul says **"us."**

JOURNAL

Using the ego vs. soul list, write down ways you could connect with your higher self rather than your ego.

1. To be of service to others. Where could you volunteer time or donate your talents for the collective good?

   _____

   _____

   _____

2. Seek inner authenticity. What behaviors will you change in order to be who you truly are?

   _____

   _____

   _____

3. See life as a gift. What are life's biggest gifts?

_____

_____

_____

_____

4. Protect. What do you feel passionate about saving, restoring, or protecting?

_____

_____

_____

_____

5. To look inward. What little changes can you make today? How can you be a better version of yourself on a daily basis?

_____

_____

_____

_____

_____

6. Feel abundance. List things that make you feel good but cannot be bought.

_____

_____

_____

_____

7. Find love. Look in places you normally would not. Journal about your findings.

_____

_____

_____

_____

8. Seek inner wisdom. Quiet your mind. What comes up?

_____

_____

_____

_____

9. Enjoy your journey. Ignite wanderlust. There is no destiny. Where will you go?

_____

_____

_____

_____

10. Embrace God. Talk to the Beloved. Cocreate with the Divine. Write to Source.

_____

_____

_____

_____

_____

11. Seek wholeness. How are you balancing body, mind, and spirit?

_____

_____

_____

_____

_____

12. Embrace everyone. Show compassion. How can you be more empathetic?

_____

_____

_____

_____

_____

"We are not human beings having a spiritual experience. We are spiritual being having a human experience."

Pierre Teilhard de Chardin, French philosopher and paleontologist

The journey to Level Six is profound. **There is an undeniable awakening that comes when you connect with Source; it is a connection you feel from within.** If your belief system has been based on organized religion where God exists outside of you, or a faith created from thought, or you do not believe in the existence of God, Level Six is an invitation to be open to the experience of feeling a connection to everything that surrounds you: every rock, tree, animal, and person. Defining your belief system gives you the opportunity to experience different perspectives and discover other levels of spiritual awareness.

JOURNAL

Define what you believe in. Take a moment and respond to your current awareness.

1. Would you define yourself as religious, spiritual, both or neither?

_____

_____

_____

_____

2. With as much detail as possible, explain your current belief system.

_____

_____

_____

_____

3. What are your thoughts about organized and collective belief systems?

     _____

     _____

     _____

     _____

4. Do you believe in God, a.k.a. Spirit, Source, the Beloved, All That Is?

     _____

     _____

     _____

     _____

     _____

5. If you do not believe in a divine intelligence, explain why.

     _____

     _____

     _____

     _____

     _____

6. What are your thoughts and theories on how life began? Where did you get the information to form your opinion?

_____

_____

_____

_____

_____

_____

_____

_____

_____

_____

_____

_____

_____

"I would say I don't believe in God but I'm afraid He might hear me."

Stephen Hawking, British theoretical physicist

" We are now ready to take another step in our understanding of God:
that God a verb.
It is not a being or thing that can be defined, rather Being expressed in and through and as everything, including you."

Mary O'Malley, author and spiritual leader

The reason you are connected to everyone and everything is because we are all made of the same ingredient-energy. What looks like a solid object, including you, are submicroscopic units of energy spinning so fast they make mass. Originally, scientists believed everything was made of matter or energy when upon a closer look, matter is mostly made of energy. In Albert Einstein's famous equation, $E = mc^2$, where energy and mass are interchangeable, the genius lies in the equal sign rather than the theory itself. Dr. Bruce Lipton explains even further in his book, *"The Honeymoon Effect"*, quantum physicists have learned that there is no physical substance inside matter. The subunits that comprise atoms are made of extremely powerful invisible energy vortices, the equivalent of nano-tornadoes, not tangible matter. Matter, as it turns out, is a strange form of energy: it is not "physical".

Without your conscious effort, nerve cells create energy in each of your organs. These nerve cells communicate with other nerve cells making them almost have their own "brain". Feeling something in your gut is an example of this phenomenon. **Thoughts, beliefs, and emotions fire up interconnecting nerve cells in your brain, emitting electrical energy that can be measured six inches outside of your head by an MRI machine**. You may have experienced a time when you "knew" what someone was thinking or going to say. According to the studies the HeartMath Institute, founded by Doc Childre, the heart produces the largest electromagnetic field of any organ in the body—sixty times the amplitude of the brain—and can be detected up to three feet away. With each person you come within just a few feet of, your circular rotating torus energies intermingle. Perhaps you have picked up on someone's "bad vibes" or "good energy". So, you are doing the same thing – giving off energy, which is generated from your thoughts. Each human being is contributing to a collective energy field. Therefore, it is imperative that you are conscious of the intentions and emotions you contribute into this field. **Your consciousness can change the world.**

Albert Einstein concluded matching frequencies creates your reality. Consider the frequencies you are exposing yourself to such as news outlets, social media, violent video games and movies, even denigrating song lyrics. Each is a frequency that you choose to tune into and will affect you on a cellular level. Western civilization is funded by consumerism, focusing on what we lack, forcing us to believe we need more. Level Six invites you to raise your vibration by expressing gratitude for what you already have. A study from the University of California, Berkley, showed that by keeping a daily gratitude journal for just three weeks reported significant better mental health in those suffering from depression and anxiety with results that lasted for 12 weeks. Focusing your attention on positive thoughts changes the molecular structure of the brain allowing you to experience improved health, mental wellness and inner peace.

EXERCISE

Start a Grateful Journal. Write just one thing you are grateful for and explain why you are grateful for it. Focus on simplicity. Begin by looking at what is right in front of you. Do this for 30 days. Note any changes in your well-being after a month of this practice.

Life's synchronicities indicate universal alignment. Being at the right place at the right time, for example. They are little signposts letting you know you are on the right track. Albert Einstein describes coincidences as God's way of remaining anonymous.

Intuition is your internal compass. Created by conscious experiences, it is a skill everyone has the ability to develop. As intuition increases, self-reliance builds along with self-respect and self-worth, allowing the highest version of yourself to emerge and create your destiny. This allows your Soul, the infinite Light of God within you, to seeks its divine purpose.

Raja yoga, the Hindu practice intended to control the mind and emotions, speaks of the Eight Powers of the Soul and elevates ruling consciousness through empowerment.

The Eight Powers of the Soul

1. The Power to Accommodate—the power to accommodate the presence, perceptions, thoughts, and ideas of others. As we adjust and accommodate these differences and stay true to ourselves, we have the opportunity to grow, become enriched; and expand ourselves through the experience brought to us by others.

2. The Power to Tolerate—the ability to remain at peace under all circumstances. By allowing our emotions to flow through us and taking a moment to regain a calm mind, we build resistance to any situation.

3. The Power to Face—to be brave enough to address all of life's problems. This power comes from knowing your truth with the intention of resolving conflicts peacefully.

4. The Power to Pack Up—the ability to bring things to an end. The decision to withdraw, end, or move on. The laws of nature are rooted in change and we must be able to adjust in order to grow.

5. The Power to Discriminate—the ability to determine what is true and what is not true. What is right and what is wrong. To know when to fight and when to walk away all to support your higher consciousness.

6. The Power to Judge—this does not mean to project judgment on others or assess a situation from a single perspective. It means assessing the quality of the words and actions of yourself and others.

7. The Power to Cooperate—the time to put attention, time, effort, experience, and wisdom in the service of others. Working toward the collective good honors you, the universe, and God.

8. The Power to Withdraw—the ability to know when to step back and detach from the world around you. The power to know your light is far brighter and separate from your physical body, the role you have created, and the responsibilities you have.

JOURNAL

Using the eight powers of the soul, write about a few of the powers
you could apply to empower your life and elevate consciousness.

———————————————————————————

———————————————————————————

———————————————————————————

———————————————————————————

———————————————————————————

———————————————————————————

———————————————————————————

———————————————————————————

"You are not in the Universe. You ARE the universe, an intrinsic part of it. Ultimately you are not a person but a focal point where the universe is becoming conscious of itself. What an amazing miracle."

Eckhart Tolle

Centering Thought

By seeing myself as separate from everything, I realize it
is my ego that keeps me disconnected from the Creator. I
surrender to the flow of life trusting divine order is at work
as it is with all living things. As my life unfolds, I will become
more aware of how everyone and everything is connected
and honor the divine spirit in all that surrounds me.

Affirmation

Today, I give myself permission to be one with the universe. Made
from stardust, my Soul is an expression of the Creator. I have
the infinite knowledge of the cosmos within me. I am a child of
the universe creating a unique human experience. I am a part
of all things – eternal and infinite. I am one with All That Is.

30 Day Grateful Journal

30 Day Grateful Journal

Level Seven

LIFE IS NOW

Present Moment Awareness

Who is reading this book right now? If your answer is, "I am" or "me", then *who* **is recognizing that there is an "I" or "me"? What part of you is acknowledging that you even exist?**

The present moment gives you the opportunity to separate from your identity and ego allowing you to experience a different version of yourself. By shifting your attention to your current surroundings with genuine interest and curiosity, feeding the ego is no longer the focus of your attention. It is difficult for the brain to do two things at the same time, such as writing an email and talking on the phone, so an attention shift creates the space for you to connect to what's going on right in front of you. Each time you choose to be present in the moment without judgment or criticism you allow yourself and others to just to *be*. Humans *be-ing*.

"I know that I exist;
The question is,
What is this "I" that "I" know."

Rene Descartes, 14th-century French philosopher,
inventor of analytic geometry

The Past and The Future.

If you are trying to live in the past because you do not like your present situation or want things to be the way they were, you will live a life of endless suffering, seeking something you will never achieve. This continued thinking will manifest into *depression* as you attempt to *create* happiness by fulfilling wants and desires rather than healing yourself and seeking inner peace. Living in the past is an attempt to re-experience feelings or a time in your life when you recall being happier, or more financially secure or having more self-worth than you do right now. Upon reflection, it is likely that at that time you were *Present, living in the moment with no thoughts about the past or concern for the future.*

Not only is the future elusive, but it does not exist because when it arrives, it *is* the present. The only "crystal ball" prediction of things to come is your current behavior, a mental path you have created in your mind, and your ego's plan to achieve it. The problem is not with planning a future. The problem is *believing* what is coming will be better than this present moment. Anticipating future happiness robs you of experiencing the present moment, your life, and the joy that surrounds you.

You can only *experience* happiness *in this moment* and there lies the power of Now.

Why be Present?

- If you live consciously in the moment, *your life won't pass you by.*
- Experiencing the present moment, such as immersing yourself in a beautiful day, will leave you feeling more gratitude and experience more joy.
- Staying Present keeps you connected to people – enhancing all human contacts as well as personal relationships.
- Focusing on the Now stops the mind from drifting to the past or thinking about the future so you spend less time experiencing worry, anxiety and depression.
- Being Present allows you to be the highest version of yourself. When you mindfully choose your words and control your behavior, you can exercise the opportunity to rise above pettiness and avoid engaging in situations that challenge your well-being.
- Attention to the aliveness around you connects you to the peace within you.

Daily Mindfulness

The layers of separation from Source are filled with wants, desires, and perceptions, just to mention a few, and are driven by basic human instincts. That is why it is important to determine what is a "want" and what is a "need". With the incessant flow of visual and audio stimulation, advertising, misinformation, opinions and perspectives that we are faced with every day, we must be aware that our unevolved brains are hardwired to feed our *desires* first. These desires create *feelings,* and those feelings guide our *actions.* The subconscious mind, the ruler and caretaker of our actions, is where all the information you received since the day you were born is stored and will gravitate toward what *feels* good. There is nothing wrong with doing or acquiring things that make you feel good and bring you joy. Traveling, hobbies, sports, games and interests challenge the mind and offer the opportunity to connect with others (or not) and requiring you to be present in the moment. Becoming mindful of *why* you need something, the *intention* behind it, and what it is you *expect* to receive by having it helps in the discernment process as the layers of separation get peeled away.

If your intention is to have a large family, then you *need* a large home. If your intention is to impress people with a grand space, then you *want* a large home. Neither scenario is good or bad, they're different, one is a *want* and one a *need*. Now is the time to determine which is which and consider what you need and want with each purchase you make. At higher levels of consciousness, the focus is placed not on how many things you acquire during your time on this planet, but rather, how little you leave behind. One of the purposes of your earth-walk is about leaving the planet a better place…simply because you existed and chose to be the best version of yourself.

"Started my day, giving away all of my baseball cards. It felt so good by the afternoon I gave some guy my car. It ain't about what you're driving or the gold you're piling. The less I have to worry about the more time I got for smiling… We try, everyone tries, tries to fit it into that ditch, can't take it when you go, never seen a hearse with a trailer hitch".

Lyrics from "Trailer Hitch", by Kristian Bush, singer, songwriter

As you detach your identity from things, the items you buy need conscious discretion. Ask yourself these questions when purchasing something.

- Do I need this or want it?
- Is it recyclable/reusable? If not, where will it end up? Who will get it next?
- Where did the item come from? How does that country contribute/harm the planet?
- What are the socio-economic conditions of the country producing the product?

Everything you purchase has a direct effect on planet earth. Reckless consumption, a lack of concern for disposal and recycling, all done mindlessly for the sake of convenience is destroying our planet. Think about how many people are randomly tossing AA, AAA, and other batteries into the garbage right now. It's illegal in the United States because batteries contain toxic material that eventually reaches a landfill that will contaminate the soil or if incinerated will pollute the air. If you mindlessly toss batteries or other toxic material into the garbage, you are contributing to the destruction of our planet so *be the change* we need to save our planet.

The marketing machine our subconscious minds are exposed to every day is in the business of *creating needs.* "You *need* this product to make you *feel* _____ ", when typically, it's a placebo with no lasting results or little to no effect. Consumerism has created a planetary *crisis* that is *inhumane* and *unsustainable* so be mindful of what you have, question what you need, and whenever possible, choose products for the wellbeing of *people* as well as the *planet.* This is one way we can heal the damage we have caused, give our brothers and sisters the opportunity to help lift themselves out of social, physical or emotional despair, and hold ourselves personally accountable for our contribution to and destruction of planet Earth.

Leaving behind a lifetime of personal memorabilia and an excess of things is *irresponsible and unfair.* The fact is nobody wants your stuff, and everything of little monetary value will probably end up in garbage bags because only *you* determine the worth of your possessions and only *you* have an attachment to them.

It can be emotionally taxing on the people who are left responsible for handling your affairs, so it stands to reason that you leave the planet with what you brought with you, nothing. Clear out your closets, get rid of your past and the things that no longer serve a purpose. Give away everything to the people and charities you intend to, and sell everything you don't *need*, NOW. Live a simple life surrounded only by what makes you happy leaving behind the essentials that are easily sold in a one-day yard sale. Give the gift of *you*. Spend *time* and *money* making *memories* for they cannot be returned, recycled, exchanged or forgotten.

Level Seven is about *being* the eternal part of you, your essence, your Soul, the Observer: not the one physically reading right now, the one *acknowledging* the reader.

Present moment awareness, the Now, requires you to know yourself beyond form. To begin to access this version of yourself, quiet and still your mind but stay alert. Free it from random, repetitive, unconscious thoughts by focusing your attention on your breath or something that is in your surroundings.

JOURNAL

Sit in stillness and quiet with no distractions. Clear your mind and focus your attention within. Contemplate before answering.

1. Where can YOU be found in your body? The answer cannot be your heart or head because as explained in this book, those two organs have specific jobs that do not require your presence so you can't be there.

_____

_____

_____

2. Write about who you are beyond form. Describe your essence, your intrinsic nature. Use your imagination. Have fun!

_____

_____

_____

3. Close your eyes and imagine a place for stillness, a place where you can always find peace under any circumstances. Describe your serene place in detail.

_____

_____

_____

4. Draw your serene place. Paper is provided at the end of Level Seven.

"God is the great mysterious motivator
of nature, and it has often been
said by philosophers that nature is
the will of God. And I prefer to
say that nature is the only body
of God that we will ever see."

Frank Lloyd Wright, American architect

You will begin to access true *inner peace* when you realize the day-to-day events, we call "life", are **designed for your spiritual growth and emotional resilience.** There is nothing to fear on this beautiful blue orb made of Divine Intelligence but your *thoughts and the situations you choose to put yourself in.* When we utilize the ego to be the driving force behind what we believe rather than succumb to the fear it creates, *we shift to our Higher Self.*

Being Present

If you have ever traveled to a place that is unfamiliar, you may have experienced present moment awareness. Different external stimuli such as sights, scents, and sounds, keep the mind curious, interested, and vigilant. It is a repetitive lifestyle and unconscious thoughts that rob you of living in the Now, so it is important to become aware of how your mind drifts and is often unaware of your surroundings.

Exercises in Present Awareness. Journal your findings.

1. Describe your surrounding with as much detail as possible.

    _____

    _____

    _____

2. With peak alertness, after you cross the threshold of a room, stop for a few minutes and become aware of the energy you feel in that space. What is calling your attention? Journal about the specific things you are drawn to.

    _____

    _____

---

3. Walk from room to room. Do you feel the same energy as you move from one to another? Journal any differences and/or similarities each room has.

---

4. When you enter a social environment, try to get a sense of the collective energy without preconceived judgements. Describe the energy of the most recent social environment you were in. Did you feel comfortable or uncomfortable? Explain why.

---

5. Spend time in a natural environment such as a park. Walk, stand or sit for a few moments and allow yourself to absorb all that surrounds you. Allow yourself to be absorbed by your surroundings. Describe, if anything, what you feel.

---

6. Spend time in a barren environment, an empty space. Do you feel a lack of energy? Can you sense any residual energy that might currently be consuming the space? Describe your findings.

_____

_____

_____

7. Experience a room with a lot of electronics. An electronics store, department or classroom that contains working computers or equipment that generates and emits electrical energy. Describe any sensations.

_____

_____

_____

How to Be in the Moment.

- Disconnect with all electronics, step away from distractions and focus your attention within. Use the heart is a focal point and allow your energy to expand from that point.
- Be alert and attentive. Train your mind to stay focused on whatever is currently happening. When it drifts to the past or future, just be aware and regain your Presence.
- Allow thoughts to flow with no attachment, judgment or criticism.
- Immerse yourself in your surroundings. Focus on sights, sounds, smells, and touch. Use them as tools when you get distracted by thought.
- Think before words leave your lips. Listen attentively when others speak. Don't overtalk. Exercise the option to be quiet.

- As emotions wax and wane allow the space for them to be and figure out their message.
- Assimilate with the Now. Relax in knowing all is well in this present moment. Connect with the natural world, its intelligence, knowing that all needs are met, including yours. With practice, this will become your natural state of *being*.

"There are only two day in the year that nothing can be done. One is called yesterday and the other is called tomorrow, so today is the right day to love, believe, do and mostly live."

The 14th Dalai Lama, Spiritual Leader of Tibet

Rising Above

Your brain does not know what is real and what is not. For example, when you watch a thriller movie, the music alone makes your heart pound. You cover your eyes, and you might even shriek in fear when *none of this is happening to you*. Your mind has convinced your body to react to the celluloid images on a flat screen perhaps to the point where you might get up and double-check an already locked door. Consciously and continuously observing what's running through your mind allows your Higher Self to scrutinize and rationalize your thought process so it can determine what is real and what is not. What is *right* and what is *wrong*.

Your mind will believe whatever you expose it to. That is why it is so important to connect with your *inner intelligence for guidance.* Begin to question the *intentions and integrity* of group thought, political affiliations, religious belief systems, and celebrities to assure they align with *your* core beliefs and values. If you follow "famous" people on social media keep in mind they have no idea, nor do they care who you are, and their *intention* is to make money by you following them. Your ego believes that because you are having an apparent direct contact with a celebrity, that you too have achieved celebrity status. This feels good-because it empowers the ego. But this is not your reality. It's their reality in which you live vicariously, and it comes with a high cost. You're *paying* to *engage* in their lives on three different levels, with your hard-earned money, your full attention and your valuable time.

Avoid people or groups that blame, shame, exclude, divide, separate, or dominate, however, examine them for the purpose of spiritual growth.

> "The universe could not exist as such if there were not some sort of equilibrium holding it together, some sort of balancing arrangement as in the spinning of the earth on its axis and the planets around the sun. A little thought will show the same principle in the just relations to human beings to the World-Mind and among themselves. Here it appears as karma."

Paul Brunton, British author of Spirituality

When you respectfully and openly accept different beliefs, ideas, opinions, and perspectives you create the space for others to act in kind. It does not matter if you agree or disagree as beliefs and opinions can change and are meant to be exchanged for a connection among our species. It is the ability to "agree to disagree", *the free-flowing exchange of diverse and different ideas that creates unity as* we contribute our unique piece to the universal puzzle. Unity creates the *whole and connects us with the Creator.* It is when we *think* we are better, worse, special, or different, we choose to *separate from the whole,* and form opinions of people that are not the same as us. Regardless of the "wrapping paper, we did not choose", we are one race, human.

Separation causes disorder. Disruption causes chaos. People or groups who cause chaos and confusion are creating victims *so they can control them.* To succumb to a group without using spiritual discretion will bring you right back to Level One, the Victim.

A truly unified group of any organized system are people who have already determined their personal beliefs. They seek like-minded thinkers who are spiritually enriched by different perspectives and are drawn together to enrich the group. People who intend to divide a group may achieve temporary power but the chaos they create generates "karma", an unbalance, that the universe sorts out as it does with all things that interfere with natural laws.

As your consciousness elevates, be mindful of the things that no longer align with your belief system. Continuous scrutiny or "spiritual pruning" is necessary on the path to inner peace as it creates the space for new concepts and beliefs to take root and flourish.

Prayer and Meditation.

Both meditation and prayer silence the mind and influence the body. Increasing the brain's ability to strengthen and improve its ability to function is one of the many health benefits of these spiritual practices. Scientific studies have shown changes in the frontal lobes of the brain in people who regularly practice meditation and prayer. There is increased activity in the cortex, the areas of the brain related to concentration and focus, during a spiritual experience. The parietal lobe, the area of the brain associated with self-awareness and the awareness of others, decreases during the same time, contributing to transcendence, an extraordinary spiritual experience. This form of spiritual transcendence can be experienced in any environment when you master inner stillness.

At Level Seven, the Higher Self rises above mundane thoughts and focuses on spiritual integrity, the quality of relationships, personal healing and wellness, and contributing to global consciousness. This is the shift from the head (thought) to the heart (feeling). From "me" to "us". *This is the subtle calling of the Beloved.*

Your thoughts will start to focus less on where you are trying to go and more on how you got here. As you align with the flow of life the need to be anything other than who you are, vanishes. Synchronicities occur, coincidences increase, and intuition begins to awaken. As you begin feel to the aliveness in you and all living things, you will recognize this connection as the *universal life force* that is generated by the Creator and connects you to all things. This is the Divine Light within you. Let that light shine. Let it light your path to inner peace.

" When you surrender
and so become fully present,
the past ceases to have any power.
The realm of Being, which has become
obscured by the mind,
then opens up.
Suddenly, a great stillness arises within you,

AN UNFATHOMABLE SENSE OF

PEACE.

And within that sense of peace,

IS GREAT JOY.

And within that great joy,

THERE IS LOVE.

And the innermost core,

THERE IS THE SACRED,
THE IMMEASURABLE
That which cannot
be named. "

Eckhart Tolle,
Spiritual leader, speaker + author

A Path to Enlightenment.

Author and Poet Shahram Shiva speaks beautifully of the "Ten Hidden Pathways to Enlightenment". His article inquires about the readiness for this journey. **Are you ready?**

- Self-Inquiry—When you begin to question your purpose and why you are here at this time, your process of self-exploration begins. Aspirations of singularity rather than group thought begin to emerge as your Soul yearns to be liberated.

- Self-Awareness—Shahram Shiva calls this the "pulse" and the single most important element in the process of enlightenment. Self-awareness taps into the psyche, intuition and instinct and runs concurrently alongside the other steps. Experience, what empowers intuition, helps your awareness which becomes more acute the longer you commit to the path.

- Self-Acceptance—With the outside bombardment of unattainable lifestyles and physical appearances, self-acceptance can be the most challenging on the path to enlightenment. Self-acceptance is achieved with an inner connection and spiritual maturity, both developed over time.

- Self-Empowerment—You alone spark the infinite trek of self-discovery. Without self-empowerment, you are just a pawn in the game of life being controlled emotionally, physically, and spiritually by outside forces.

- Self-Worth—The greatest gift you can bestow upon yourself; and, since you are stuck with yourself for all of eternity, the sooner you love and respect yourself the better.

- Self-reliance—You are a unique spark following you own intuition. Let your Soul guide you as you develop faith in yourself and develop resilience to change.

- Self-Healing—Care for your body, mind, and spirit. Reconnect with your natural ability to heal and find ways to assist it. Maintaining a healthy weight, eating natural food, and getting plenty of exercise and rest supports the immune system, your healing system.

- Self-Love—An impossibility for most as many cannot stand being alone so they will settle for soul-draining relationships. Moving beyond shame and guilt and loving the person you are right now without needing acceptance from anyone else is how you build self-love.

- Self-Guided Destiny—You are the guide, the torch, the Sherpa, the Lord, Messiah, the twists and the turns. The journey to enlightenment is uniquely yours—it's all about you.

- Enlightenment—Takes a mind thirsty for growth, a spirit that never settles, a psyche that constantly questions everything, and a good amount of discipline to stay motivated and focused. It takes a spark that wants to celebrate its uniqueness.

" DO NOT GO WHERE THE PATH MAY LEAD RATHER, GO INSTEAD WHERE THERE IS NO PATH AND LEAVE A TRAIL".

RALPH WALDO EMERSON,
TRANSCENDENTALIST, PHILOSOPHER, AND POET

Tips for the journey

- Give up all resistance.
- Surrender to the flow of life.
- Identify the things you can change and accept everything else as it is.
- Rise above the temptation for material things that feed the ego to create a sense of worth.
- Live a simple life. Take care of your health, exercise your body and heal it with fresh water. healthy food and adequate rest.
- Control your thoughts so your fears and desires are not the driving force of your existence.
- Become the observer of your thoughts and feelings and let them go without judgment.
- Create a quiet place within you so you always have a place to connect with the Beloved.
- Let your light shine brightly as it will light a path for others.
- Smile, wave, and keep walking...

Centering Thought

Like the rays of the sun, I am an extension of the Creator.
An energetic being that is perfect, whole, and complete.
Choice is my only power in human form and my choices
affect the vibration of the universe. Using consciousness as
my guide, I need to be nothing more than who I am.
Being the change, I want to see in the world, seeking
the beauty in everyone and everything, and living
life as the most exquisite version of myself
is how I express my divinity.

Affirmation

I am Light.
I am Love.
I am Divine

"And suddenly you know:
It's time to start something new
and trust the magic of beginnings."

Meister Eckhart, 13th century Dominican mystic.

The Beginning

ACKNOWLEDGMENTS OF LOVE

Let them see You through me. My eternal love
& devotion to Big G. I hope I got it right.
"Coffee Boy", "Mr. Thatcher", my husband and endless
love, David John Simmons. Thanks for the nonstop
supply of caffeine and never doubting me.
Brie, my lovely Assistant, thank you for never leaving my side.
My editing team, Candace Moore, thank you for your
advice, experience, effort and support. Michele and
Wesley Whiteman, you saved me from making a complete
asterisk out myself. I am forever in your debt.
Kelly Brunetti Costa, thank you for making this dream come true.
My Girl Posse (in alphabetical order). I could not
have done this with your love and support.
Johanna Baccan, Sangeeta Banerjee, Tonti Cline, Lori
Franco, Cora Gabriel, Valerie Giarusso, Carol Hall,
Linda Inganamort, and Kathy MacFarlane.
To beloved family - Samantha, Michael, Wolfgang James,
Sebastian Moon and Quin Maxwell. Jessica, Mark, Ruby
June and Madelyn Rae. Thank you for teaching me
everything I know about love. Because of you…
Aham Prema

Printed in the United States
by Baker & Taylor Publisher Services